HAL•LEONARD INSTRUMENTAL PLAY-ALONG

AUDIO ACCESS INCLUDED

PLAYBACK+
Speed • Pitch • Balance • Loop

T0088324

VIOLIN

Worship Favorites

CONTENTS

To access audio visit:
www.halleonard.com/mylibrary

1431-5572-3970-2028

ISBN 978-1-4234-9936-7

HAL•LEONARD®
7777 W. BLUEMOUND RD. P.O. BOX 13819 MILWAUKEE, WI 53213

Visit Hal Leonard Online at
www.halleonard.com

AGNUS DEI

VIOLIN

Words and Music by
MICHAEL W. SMITH

EVERLASTING GOD

VIOLIN

Words and Music by BRENTON BROWN
and KEN RILEY

GREAT IS THE LORD

VIOLIN

Words and Music by MICHAEL W. SMITH
and DEBORAH D. SMITH

Moderately Fast

HE IS EXALTED

VIOLIN

Words and Music by
TWILA PARIS

HERE I AM TO WORSHIP

VIOLIN

Words and Music by
TIM HUGHES

HOSANNA
(Praise Is Rising)

VIOLIN

Words and Music by PAUL BALOCHE
and BRENTON BROWN

With a driving beat

HOW MAJESTIC IS YOUR NAME

VIOLIN

Words and Music by
MICHAEL W. SMITH

IN CHRIST ALONE

VIOLIN

Words and Music by KEITH GETTY
and STUART TOWNEND

INDESCRIBABLE

VIOLIN

Words and Music by LAURA STORY
and JESSE REEVES

LEAD ME TO THE CROSS

VIOLIN

Words and Music by
BROOKE FRASER

MIGHTY TO SAVE

VIOLIN

Words and Music by BEN FIELDING
and REUBEN MORGAN

With praise

THE POWER OF THE CROSS
(Oh to See the Dawn)

VIOLIN

Words and Music by KEITH GETTY
and STUART TOWNEND

Slowly, with freedom

molto rit.

STILL

VIOLIN

Words and Music by
REUBEN MORGAN

THERE IS A REDEEMER

VIOLIN

Words and Music by
MELODY GREEN

THE WONDERFUL CROSS

VIOLIN

Words and Music by JESSE REEVES,
CHRIS TOMLIN and J. D. WALT